TH HERBERTS OF DORCHESTER
AND THEIR STEAM

By Kay Townsend

Front cover by clare@createabilitystudio.co.uk

MEMORY LANE

*THIS BOOK WILL CONTAIN TRUE STORIES AND
ACCOUNTS
THAT SHOULD NOT BE LOST, BUT WRITTEN FOR THE
FUTURE GENERATION TO KNOW*

INTRODUCTION

The Herbert family yard, is only ten miles from us and being showmen, Herberts and Townsends have opened and work together many times over the years.

David Herbert in his latter years, would love telling me about his family, then in May 2011 at the age of 86 David Herbert passed away. Although I was only able to see him about twice a year, the moment he was gone I knew I would miss our laughter and his stories. To leave his stories in a file unseen would be a shame, as his future generation will one day ask all about the HERBERTS.

So to the family I say, here are your stories, hold them close and they will never leave you.

Thank you to Edward and Lewis Herbert, as with-out their help to complete, this book would not have been possible.

So here we go, down memory lane.

This book is in memory of David George Herbert

1924 – 2011

We will start in 1800s, when John William Herbert was a respectable horse dealer, trading between here and Ireland mainly in shire horses for the brewery trade. John had three children. His son Tom became the proprietor of 'Sunny Dean Garages' and shops of Leicestershire.

His daughter married the owner of a Butcher shop, but this story will follow his son born in 1872, John Henry (Jack) Herbert.

John made sure Jack had a good education, but Jack decided not to follow a career putting his education to good use, instead he decided to follow his father by attending the street/cattle fairs, not to trade horses, but with a Joy Wheel, to give people rides at the street fairs.

Remember we are talking late 1800s so rides were primitive, but the object of the ride was to stay on, as riders would one by one fall off, bear-in mind there were no health & Safety.

Looking at the photo above, the thrill here is the anticipation that any moment the wheel would start to turn and they knew they would be hanging on to each other in desperation to stay on, with one or two screams along the way. Then when they did fall off, the indignity of showing their normally covered legs and having to adjusting their attire while others watch, only here could you be so daring in a public place.

Jack's mind for business he got from his father, as from a young man Jack was making a good living.

Next to follow was marriage and in Jack's case a reasonable size family, fathering his last child at 60.

Jack's first wife was Miss Sally Newman, a showman's daughter thought to be from the midlands. Sally gave him a family of five children John, Jimmy, Frank, Annie and

Marshall

Jack made enough money with his Joy wheel over a period of time to buy a live shooter stall, which Sally would look after, also they had a snake show which little Annie's job was to look after the snakes and during the show would wrap the snakes around her. The large tea chests/boxes to pack the prizes in, Jack made separate compartments at the bottom, with a little flap door and this was for storing the snakes. To keep them warm in the winter, the snakes were kept in the living wagon locker next to the bed.

He also bought two round stalls, one with 'Wheel-em in (roll the penny) and one with ring over the block (Hoopla). The couple were travelling by horses at this time and doing so well that money from the hoopla stall, bought Jack his first traction engine.

Until 1909, Jack like other showmen the horse had been their pulling power on the road. Then 25th February 1909, Jack bought his first traction engine. Engine 3063 was brand new from Burrells of Thetford. She came in crimson red with yellow wheels.

He named the engine *Houpla*, after the ring and blocks Hoopla stall, that earnt the money to buy the engine.

Brand new and ready to go
Road Loco Society

What's in a name?

You will note the spelling of the engines name a *Houpla*. Traditionally the word is spelt Hoopla, referring to a showman's round stall, We are unsure why it was spelt as *Houpla*. Maybe the man who cast the name plate made the mistake.

Sadly his wife, Sally passed away at the age of 34.
In 1914 at the age of 42, Jack re married.

Photo from granddaughter Lesley Searle
His second wife was Miss Mildred Moore.

Mildred was 22 years younger then him.
They met whilst Jack was staying at Locks showman's yard, Bedminster, Bristol.
Mildred's family originally from Spain, settled in Meveggissey, Cornwall and for a number of years making a living from the pilchard fleet, her family were now settled in Bristol.
Jack had only known Mildred three months and told her, *"I would like to marry you, but I'm moving to Winchester to do Government work with the engine."* Mildred thought on Jacks words of marriage and she caught a train to Winchester to accept his proposal.
Jack had secured the contract to do haulage to Winchester Army barracks on behalf of the War Department, and was working on the engine with a man called Abraham Day. So Jack did not travel during this period and stayed in a yard that belong to showman John Wall at Bar End, the Wall family were also doing haulage work with their engine.

Jack's eldest sons from his first marriage, John and Frank, were called up for the Army. Frank was wounded whilst in France and consequently Frank was discharged, he was shot through his left side near his lung, leaving him with a withered hand.

DENNIS

It was 1915 and Frances Dennis Monaghan was 14, Jack was busy at the time with the engine working in Winchester for the War Department, when Dennis asked Jack if he could help. Dennis's father had died and he did not get on with his new stepfather, so helping Jack got Dennis away from the house. When the war ended and Jack was going to start travelling again, he asked Dennis what he was going to do now! Dennis said, *"I want to travel with you Mr Herbert"*.

Jack asked Dennis's mother if he could and he was told yes if you look after

him, which he did, as Dennis remained with the Herberts for the rest of his life and was like a member of the family.

This photo are just some children from both marriages.
The woman holding small child (Ruby), is Nellie White, a Nanny in their employ to help look after the children.

With WWI now over, travelling got back to normal.
This photo shows Mildred on the left with Jack. Taken c1921, with baby Ruby being two years. The couple here had been married about six years.

Jack and Mildred had 11 children, Doris, Tommy, Ruby, Evelyn, Bernard, David, Stanley, Edward, Henry, Lewis, and Jean bringing Jack's total to 16 children. Mealtimes were usually a sitting of three children at a time.

When WWI had ended, travelling resumed And young Frank despite his hand was given the job of looking after the engine *Houpla.*

Baby Ruby becomes a beautiful young lady

THEN THERE WAS BELLA

Years ago it was not unusual for a circus to open along with a fair.
On one of these occasions a circus opened with Jack, but business was poor and the circus did not do very well. At the end the circus proprietor said,
"Mr *Herbert Im sorry but have not taken enough to give you the rent",*
Jack felt sorry for the man, who happen to have a foul born in the circus, her name was 'Bella' and was destined for the circus ring. It is unsure if Jack took the pony in lou of rent, or he gave £5 for her. Although Jack was raised in and around the horse trade, he did not part with Bella, in fact he became attach to the horse and she became more like a family pet.
'Bella' had watched her mother perform in the ring and never forgot, as when the fairground organ music started, Bella would dance around as if she was in the ring.

As the family grew up, Jack needed more income so, around 1920, he bought his first big ride, a 'galloper' horses roundabout, from Edward Forrest of Burford, Oxfordshire.

The ride manufacturer was Walkers of Tewksbury in 1888.
Photo FHT collection

This photo was taken some years before Jack bought it and shows it in good working order but the ride now needed much work doing before Jack could travel it again. New parts were made by Andersons of Bristol and included carved wooden cockerels and 32 horses. The first wooden horse was sent in a large box by train, with the remaining order following two or three at a time as they were being made. New rounding boards and swifts were also made for the top and one row of steps for the bottom. Surprisingly, the platforms, which are prone to rot, were in good order.

Example only
*Photos above (courtesy of Fairground Heritage Trust,
Patrick Chivers collection*

The steam centre-engine needed renewing, so he eventually replaced it by installing an electric motor in the centre of the roundabout. However, the starter was placed in the coal tender on the back of the traction engine, so one man could stoke the engine and turn the ride on. Another man would collect the fares and hand them to Jack, who was sometimes minding the penny slot machines. He would count the riders as the Gallopers turned and the money-taker would be told if he forgot one!

Taken at Verwood

In the centre of the ride was a barrel organ which only played eight tunes. One day, another showman offered to tow the organ truck for Jack but, somehow, it tipped over, fell into a ditch and was so damaged it never played

properly again. Instead, Jack played organ music from records on a "Panatrope" which was an early electrically-amplified gramophone and speakers. The barrel organ was put into store until one Christmas when Jack had very little to give his children, so he gave them a brass horn each from the old instrument. His children thought it was great fun running around the yard, blowing and making a racket! A few years later, as Edward had found rats were nesting in the organ, Jack

told young Edward to pull it into the centre of the yard and burn it. (More on their yard later)

The organ had a Bandmaster and beautiful bell-ringer figures mounted on the front but these, sadly, were not taken off.

BUSY YEAR FOR BUYING ENGINES

When Jack bought the Gallopers, in 1920, he needed another engine, as *Houpla* alone was not enough to tow everything he now had, which was Swingboats, Overboats, stalls and now the Galloper trucks along with two living-wagons. In 1921, eleven years after Jack bough *Houpla,* he bought two more engines.

Jack's second engine was also brand new. Burrell no.3890 arrived in March 1921 by goods train, with her canopy on a separate truck which was fitted on arrival.

At this time he was wintering at the Deanery in Southampton where he and Mildred would stroll along the docks admiring the ships. They noticed one liner called *Majestic* and that's when he decided to name his new engine with the same name. Dennis was now 21 years old and Jack gave him the responsibility of looking after the new engine.

Photo Cliff Austin

The next engine Jack purchased was *St Bernard*, Burrell no.3192, which was new to the War Department on June 1st, 1910 complete with a front crane and it had been working at Chatham. In 1921, as the engine was now eleven years old, the Government Dept decided to sell it

James Gilbey collection
Example photo, however, due to the position of the chain driven governors
this could well be *St Bernard*.

St Bernard was converted to a showmans engine and was needed to tow the living-wagon, so this was her main job and she was driven for a number of years by Jack's eldest son from his second marriage, Tommy.

On one of these occasions, when Tommy and David were travelling the engine, Tommy was so tired that he stopped the engine and had an hour's sleep on the grass verge. When continuing their journey and trying to make up for lost time, they were pulled over by the police for speeding. In addition, the officer also discovered Tommy had no licence and David was too young to drive!

When travelling through Gillingham, Dorset, a shop keeper called to the driver of the *Majestic* as she was passing, *"where is Tommy and St Bernard?,"* the reply was, *"not far behind!"*. The shop keeper quickly got his pole and pushed in his outside blind. Apparently, *St Bernard* hit the blind when passing previously and the shop keeper was taking no chances.

Lesley Searle

St Bernard was needed to tow the living wagon, so this was *St Bernard's* main job and was driven for a number of years by Jack's eldest son from his second marriage, Tommy.

James Gilbey Collection

On one occasion when Tommy and David were with the engine, Tommy was so tired he stopped the engine and had an hours sleep on the grass verg. When continuing their journey and trying to make up for lost time, they were pulled over by the police for speeding. The officer also discovered Tommy had no licence and David was too young to drive.

A NEW HOME

Until 1926, Jack's winter base was The Deanery, Southampton then, in 1927, he spent the winter in Kings Road, Dorchester, Dorset (where the Swan pub now is). Here, Jack discovered a builder named Slade who owned a piece of land on which was a disused flax mill, in St Georges Road, Dorchester. Mr Slade had money problems and could not develop the land. In 1928, Jack bought the plot and it became his new winter quarters, complete with a building to store and re-decorate his rides. Jack's first child born in their new home was Edward.

THE RUNWAY

It was about 1930, as the family were travelling through the east-Somerset village of Milborne Port, when *Houpla* had an unfortunate accident. The main road had a slight incline and yards before the engine entered the village, *Houpla* was stopped to be put into low gear before proceeding. But, with no block to stop her, suddenly the engine started to roll.

Stopping point with a deceiving incline

16

The driver desperately tried to put her in gear whilst she was rolling, then realising he would never do it, fear struck him on this rattling out of control engine.

As the law then permitted, the family could ride in their living-wagon and Mildred and the children were in it!

The steersman shouted to *"Get the children out of the living wagon, quick!"*. He stayed with the engine and was commended afterwards for not jumping off. Mildred started to hand her children out from the wagon door, one by one, to one of the enginemen as the wagon was slowly moving along.

However, *Houpla* started to gain speed, until it was too fast to hand the children out of the door any longer.

The road that confronted the steersman was 'Samson Hill'

This view below from opposite direction.

With four children still with her, Bernard, David and two daughters, Mildred ran to the bedroom and covered herself and the children with their eiderdown bedspread. She was screaming loudly with such fear at this point that the children were now crying and frightened.

Bridge wall on right of photo

17

At the time, Townsends, were open with their fair in a field near the main road. They said they could hear *Houpla* coming as she rattled past them down the road and they realised something was wrong.

Meanwhile, *Houpla* clipped a cart belonging to Jack Isaacs, a showman who was travelling with them. *Houpla* came to a stop when she hit a bridge wall! Meanwhile, Jack Isaacs' head slowly appeared from behind a garden wall and was, thankfully, uninjured, however, red paint he was carrying, was spilt all over the place.

Several men from Townsend's came running to help. The trauma was over and, thankfully, everyone was fine and they gathered around the engine to assess the damage. Repairs were made by a local blacksmith before they could continue. Mildred and the children were, happily, unscathed, but that fearful day remained with her and she suffered with nervousness for many years after.

PROBLEMS ON THE ROAD

Travelling on narrow country lanes were common place, as fairs would often open in small villages for country shows.

Fairs were then a big attraction and caused much excitement in the surrounding villages. Young Eddie would ride on a board as brake-boy on the last truck being towed. He would tug at a long line leading to a bell on *Majestic* telling the steersman a car needed to pass. In the early years, Jack's children were too young to ride on the board and he was once stopped by the police for not having a brakeman on one truck being towed. They also found he had no safety chain between the engine and truck.

Travelling through one of those narrow country lanes, during a storm, at the side of the road was a high earth bank and the rain was so bad, it washed away the bank allowing a large rock to fall into the road. *Majestic* was only a few feet away from it when it happened with Dennis steering the engine, but he did not see the rock ahead of them. *Majestic* mounted this large rock and with a crash, she dropped back onto the road surface, it snapped the rear axle. The engine was jacked up and the broken part was removed. The engine's crew were working in heavy rain and mud, as earth had washed down across the narrow lane. They contacted Burrell's at Thetford for a new back axle to be sent immediately and soon it arrived at nearby Pen Mill railway station in Yeovil.

Jack Herbert collected the part with Bella and her trap. Unfortunately the axle proved to be far too heavy for Bella so rope was wrapped around the trap, trying to keep it all together. The wheels were leaning out at an alarming angle and poor Bella was struggling with the weight. It has been said this horse had a lovely temperament and she always behaved perfectly. Even though it was far too great a load for her, she had 15 miles to pull the trap before reaching *Majestic*. The engine stood on the roadside for over a week before she was ready to steam again.

Family photo

You have seen a hard working family, but the public back then rarely appreciated what show families went through to bring a fair to the town. Fairs could also have a mixed reception, as one day a local man reported the engine for speeding.

Majestic's water hose was a little short for filling her tank at some rivers and streams.

On the main A36 road into Salisbury is a bridge over the river Wylye and a warning plated on it stated that locomotive wheels were not to encroach on the structure or a £5 penalty (£250 by 2012 values!) would be imposed. However, with *Majestic's* hose being a little short, they had no option but for her front wheels to be slightly on the bridge. Unfortunately, a police officer passing by was not so understanding and imposed the £5 fine, which Jack had to pay!

Majestic needed a new wire spark-catcher on her chimney, as hot sparks ejecting from steam engines were a common problem. When driving along the Cranborne road, heading to Verwood, a stray spark landed on a hay stack and set it ablaze!

BUT THE WORSE WAS YET TO COME

It was in the Spring of around 1933 and the Herberts had just taken on a new man to help Dennis with *Majestic*. Dennis said he lent over just to check the fire box was ok but, as he stood up, the engine was already going over. It is thought the new man misjudged the road, steering her towards the bank. The family were on their way to Maiden Newton and the *St Bernard* had already arrived at the field when Jack and Mildred arrived with Bella. Mildred broke the news to the rest of the family: *"MAJESTIC HAS GONE OVER!"*

Ron Dawe Road Loco society

Photo, Ron Dawe

The truck in this photo is where the wooden Galloper horses were packed. As the engine went over, the new man fell over the side and downwards, the rear wheel trapping his leg. This field know as the 'Wear', has a river and is also often waterlogged. Even the ditch was full of water that day.

When the fire brigade arrived they used sand bags to create a dam, then drained the ditch of its water and, much to their surprise, they managed to free the man saving his leg. Next, they set to work moving away the loaded trucks, etc.

Ron Dawe Road Loco Society

Her twisted brass is bent, the site now clear to start getting her upright. Seeing how flat the engine is lying and with the water beneath, we can only imagine how terrified the trapped man must have been. Planks were needed to cross this wide ditch.

The family tried to up-right *Majestic* themselves, by jacking her up a little at a time, but, after a week and the road still closed off, they were getting nowhere. With the family at the end of their tether with the situation, Jack called on a local garage owner, a Mr Perkins, who was known for helping the railway when carriages had derailed. He was asked if he could help, as they had tried everything and did not know what to do next. Mr Perkins agreed to help on the condition they respected his word. He gathered all his equipment, which included chain block, jacks, sleepers, and two tree posts. He gave everyone instructions that everything had to be done his way or he would walk away.

Ron Dawe, Road loco Society
The canopy had to be cut away before work could start.

Photo Lesley Searle

Cab of *Majestic* is now off, as it would have been in the way for the lifting gear.

Now with chain block and jacks, she could slowly be pulled upright with help from two tree posts inserted in the ground acting as stills, supporting the chain block.

Houpla was on opposite side of the road acting as anchor and *St Bernard* was running back and forth with the timber/sleepers. As *Majestic* rose inch by inch, the winch rope leading across the road to *Houpla* was tightened. The road was closed for a total of three weeks.

Jack at the back of engine looking on.
Photo Lesley Searle

Thankfully the accident happened not far from their yard. Here she is back in St Georges Road. Although the photo is not good, we can see the wheels are on three sleepers as men try to get her ready for the road again

ANOTHER SMALL MISHAP

I don't know what it is about Milborne Port but, in 1939, when passing through the village again, one of their engines suddenly veered right into a wall. No real damage was done and it is thought a steering chain snapped. Everything stopped while the men decided what to do. Eddie was 11 years old and was holding on to Bella whilst the men sorted out the engine. A local man was passing with a yolk across his shoulders carrying two pails of water. With steam travel being slow and now with this set back, it was a long hot day for Bella, so Eddie asked the man, *"Can I have some water for my horse please?"*. The man said *"I got no water for your horse"* and went to join the men at the front of the engine. He then decided to tell Jack what he should do to get the engine away from the wall. We can only presume he was giving poor advice, as Jack told him to go away!

The engine was jacked-up, the front axle turned straight again and the chain was rejoined by a nut and bolt. Soon, they were on their way again and, as this temporary repair held fast, that bolt remained in place for a number of years.

THE REPLACMENT

Jack spent a lot of money and effort to get the Gallopers as he wanted them but, by this time, with it being a slow ride, they were going out of favour and he said he regretted buying them.

Britain's first Dodgem car ride was set up at Blackpool's permanent fairground in 1921 and by 1928 Dodgems suitable for travelling showmen were being imported from the USA. With the roaring success of these rides, Jack could see that this was the attraction to have and, in 1935, he bought a second-hand set from the Scottish showmen, White's.

Due to the distance involved, Jack did not view them before buying and they were delivered to Dorchester by goods train. His new Dodgems were a 'square track' version made by Lang Wheels of Uxbridge, Middlesex. Once he'd opened them, Jack saw that the fairgoers wanted to ride the Dodgems and that the Gallopers were not doing so well as they had, so he decided to retire the old roundabout and stored it at St Georges Road.

For the next five years he travelled the Dodgems around Dorset, Somerset and Devon, until September 3rd 1939. On that day, Jack was pulling into the north Dorset village of Melbury Osmond, for the local flower show, when the police informed him that war had just been declared between Britain and Nazi Germany and he was advised to return home. With the season having come to an abrupt end, the Dodgems were put under cover in St Georges Road along with the retired Gallopers.

OPEN AGAIN

In 1940, the Government introduced 'Holiday At Home Fairs' to help boost the morale of the nation. Jack was invited to open his fair on the Fairfields car park, Dorchester to bring a little pleasure and help people forget the worries of war. As the fairground looked rather sparse, he brought the Gallopers out again, which gave him two rides open in the town. We can only presume the gallopers still did not do well next to the dodgems, as in 1941, Jack sold the Gallopers to Jack. Rose, of London. Once again, it was just the Dodgems. From 1943, sometimes Townsends would come from Weymouth to join them for a few weeks.

Eventually, Jack Herbert's Gallopers went to Butlin's holiday camp at Hayling Island, Hampshire before being sold to America where, sadly, they were scrapped in the late 1950s.

GOOD-BY HOUPLA

Road Loco Society

Before World War II started, the boiler failed on *Houpla*. She was parked in the yard at St Georges Road until some scrap dealers, hunting metal for munitions, called in. Scrap metal for the war effort was so badly needed that buyers were scouting for miles to find it, so much so, in Jack's case, that the dealers had travelled 50 miles from Romsey, Hampshire. Jack sold her for just £1 per ton, which totalled £12, (£1,500 by 2012 values) plus a little extra for the brasswork. The men returned and cut up *Houpla* in the yard and took her away in pieces, but they forgot to take one part - her tool box, which is still in the yard to this day.

As Jack's fair was open in the car park, two Military officials and two Dorchester town Councillors visited St Georges Road and said they wanted to use it for storage of military vehicles. Jack said no to this, so one of the councillors took Jack to one side and said, *"Look Jack, we must use your land for something, how about turning it into a piggery" ?* Jack agreed to this. A nearby farmer, Mr Reed, gave him advice on keeping pigs. Jack's sons Eddie and Stanley looked after the farm. So with *Houpla* gone for scrap, Herbert's yard was well and truly empty and soon became home for 1,000 pigs, chickens and ducks!

Meanwhile, in the Market car park, as with all Dodgem tracks, the floor plates needed repair or replacing. Being war time, Jack could not believe his luck when a local engineering firm, Lotte & Walne, supplied him with two 8 foot by 4 foot steel sheets. Unfortunately, it was not carbon steel and was too soft for the heavy Dodgem cars wear and tear. Over time, the two floor plates began wearing thin, as the steel was being rolled outwards by the weight of the car, so often the edges overlapped and had to be filed back.

One night, whilst powering the dodgems, *Majestic's* dynamo burnt out. Townsends, who were open with them at the time, powered everything with their Fowler engine *Queen Mary* until *Majestic* was repaired.

As there was no travelling for Jack during the war years, his horse, Bella, was having a quiet time, apart from the Bofors gun which was used to shoot at enemy aircraft and sited near the rides. One night, as the gun blazed, Bella broke her chain with fright but, fortunately, Edward managed to catch her and calm her down.

No matter what, the Dodgems opened all year round. By the end of the war in 1945, the ride's base which was made from wood, urgently needed replacing. As there were timber shortages, due to wartime materials rationing, the wood was accumulated over a long period. When enough had been collected, a new base for the floor plates was made. However, the wood had not been seasoned and, with time, the wood warped and sagged, causing the track to develop dips, and it had to be replaced again.

As the market still took place on Wednesdays, young Eddie would collect wooden apple and orange boxes from the market, to light *Majestic's* fire. Also his daily chore was to clean *majestic's* brass, using a ladies long cotton sock.

WAR OVER

When V.E. Day was announced (Victory in Europe), Jack and the Townsends decided to open at the Bridport May Fair. Whilst there, they heard that Dorchester was now full of home-coming troops so, after the fair was over, the families decided to return to Dorchester again instead of travelling on. However, *Majestic* was not well. David and Dennis were with the engine and told Tom Townsend that they had doubts she would make it up Stony Head Hill. It was agreed that Tom would go in front with *Queen Mary* and, if *Majestic* did not make it, Tom would come back for them. Sure enough, *Majestic* only managed to climb half way up the hill. Tom slowly reversed *Queen Mary* down the hill to hook up Herbert's engine and trucks.

Imagine, if you will, the load now consisted of *Queen Mary* 22 feet 6 inches (6.8m), an 8 foot (2.4m) straight bar, *Majestic* 19 feet 10 inches (6m), and two trucks averaging 29 feet each (8.83m), including tow bars, and water dandy. The total length was now an incredible 129 feet!

Queen Mary, Fowler 15319

With the ending of WWII, ex-military vehicles came up for auction in Oxfordshire. Jack sent for a catalogue and of the six Mack trucks on the list, three caught Jack's eye; two had once been for civilian use but all were now ex-Army.

He bid for the first and when the hammer came down, he was asked how many do you want, he said, "*I'll take all six*". He sold two; one of these went to Bristol showman Henry Rogers, one he scrapped, and three he kept for himself. Being ex tank transporters and were 36 feet long, a 16ft sectioning was cut form the lorry to make it a tractor. One was returned to a Mack supplier and had a diesel engine fitted. They did not make a good job of it, as it was installed out of line with the gearbox and was forever breaking the clutch plates.

The two remaining lorries had petrol engines which returned just over three miles per gallon! Fuel was still on ration at the time and this did not end until September 1950.

What are smoke engines?

These special engines burned oil and were made to produce thick smoke to conceal areas such as airfields from the view of enemy aircraft flying over. Three ship-style chimneys on top of each engine produced thick smoke very quickly and, if there was more than one in any area, they were very effective. Jack bought three smoke engines which were mounted on flat trailers but he really only needed each trailer's chassis. Each trailer was about 18 ft long and 7ft wide.

Again, these came from the auction sale near Oxford.

Driving the Mack, it took three days to get back to Dorchester and two of the vehicles had no round couplings to pin the trucks together, so young David Herbert rigged up two temporary ones, just to get them home.

Travelling at a steady ten miles per hour, they had reached Newbury when police pulled them over to ask what was on the trailers. They said, *"Smoke engines."* The officer said he had not seen anything like it before and, because of the three funnels on each, they looked like ships on wheels. Everyone burst into laughter, as they could see his point!

When Jack and David reached Salisbury they called in to see a show family named Baker, who had ceased travelling due to the war. The Baker's had acquired some old railway 'sleeping' carriages and were now letting them out to drivers passing through. Jack and young David stopped overnight in

31

one of the carriages. The next day it started to snow so chains were fixed around the Mack wheels for better grip on the road. With only 40 miles to go, the back truck started to sway all over the road, as one of the temporary coupling rings had loosened. They had to pull over again and, by now, it was bitterly cold. Travelling at 10 mph they decided to give up as being on the road three days now they had just about had enough.

They left the three trailers at the roadside and drove the Mack on to Dorchester. They went back the next day to try again and this time completed the job. After getting the trailers home, the smoke engines were sold for scrap and Jack made use of the chassis.

THE PASSING OF 'BELLA'

During the winter months after WWII had ended, Jack and his sons would fell trees on the Ilchester estate, on the A37 Dorchester to Yeovil road.

So they would know which trees were to be cut down, a red line was painted on the chosen trees by the estate's manager.

By this time, Jack's pony, Bella, had been part of the family for 25 years and she was with them whilst they were working on the estate. Then she started to lose weight as she was unable to eat. The vet said due to her age, best thing to do was put her to sleep. Jack had owned the horse since it was a foal and asked the farmer if he had somewhere they could bury her.

The farmer pointed across a field where, under some trees, he did not plough and they were welcome to bury her there. Tommy, Dennis and David dug her grave but being it was winter, the ground was very hard.

The farmer placed two hurdles behind his tractor so, as Bella fell, she landed on them. Her body was pulled across the field on the hurdles by tractor, lowered into her grave, then covered with cloth before being buried. In later years, the new generation who did not know her, talked of how she never made it to the circus ring but would dance to the music of their fairground organ.

Jack and Bella

Photo Lesley Searle

Herbert's engines were well known and, perhaps, in the latter days you may remember seeing this family travelling to:

Hazelbury Bryan Flower Show

Queen Camel, Somerset

Martinstown, Street fair, Dorchester

Wyke Regis, Weymouth.

Shaftesbury Fair

Fontmell Magna, Shaftesbury

Nunney Catch,

Sixpenny Handley

Yetminster, and Stoke Under Ham, Somerset

Jack wanted to open at Easton, on the top of Portland, but Mildred would not allow it, due to the steep climb to the top of the island. The runaway years before hand, at Milborne Port had taken its toll

A MAJESTIC LIFE

Now the family had lorries, it was time to say good by to steam. *Houpla* was long gone and these two had worked hard keeping everything on the road.

Majestic and *St Bernard*

Majestic was retired the end of the 1947 season and stood in their Dorchester yard until 1954, when she was sold to Mr T G Hunt of Oldbury, near Birmingham. His son, Bill Hunt travelled to Dorchester to view the engine, despite it snowing and being bitterly cold, he recalled later. When viewing her, he decided she was worthy of restoration and, consequently, his father purchased *Majestic*.

Below we see *Majestic* with dynamo off, ready to leave St Georges Road

Road Loco society

Majestic was taken to Hunt Brothers foundry at Oldbury. Mr Hunt senior had *Majestic* and his son Bill, purchased her sister engine, Burrell 3910, *Wait and See*, which had to be rescued from the scrap yard. By the way, *Majestic* towed *Wait and See* from the scrap yard, however on the way home her fire bars dropped. Father and son thought they could make one good engine from both but, fortunately, this didn't happen and both engines are still with us..

In 1948, Jack had bad circulation in his feet and was confined to his bed. In 1949, when the family were open at Brook Water, near Shaftesbury, Dorset, Jack passed away. His final words were to his son, Lewis, *"Here they come"* and he closed his eyes forever. We are not sure what he meant by this; maybe he saw the light as his death was approaching. Jack Herbert was 77.

His wife and children continued the business.

Mildred survived her husband by 34 years, passing away 1983.

Their grandchildren continue the tradition and the family lives on.

James Gilbey collection
I mentioned earlier when young David and Tommy were pulled over with *St Bernard* for speeding, Tommy had no licence, and David was too young to drive her.
This is Tommy, with the engine in the ownership of James Gilbey from nearby Compton Pauncefoot.

Photo John Reeves
In the summer of 2010, at 85 years old, David was also reunited with *St Bernard* at Abbey Hill Rally, Yeovil

ACKNOLEGMENTS

Thank you to,
Eddie and Lewis Herbert
Lesley Searle for photos
Shane Seagrave for proof reading
Fairground Heritage Trust
Mr Bill Hunt for Majestic history
Caroline Herbert for photo enhancement
Any photos not credited are from the family's collection or are owned by the author

MY OTHER PUBLICATIONS

Something you may have given little thought to is what happened to the fairgrounds during World War II.

How did they survive this awful time?

On the day Britain went to war against Nazi Germany, in September 1939,

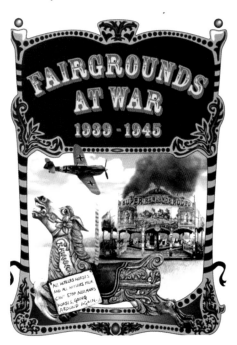

police went to the fairgrounds and closed them down. During the early months of the conflict there was little military action and this time was called "The Phoney War". This quiet period drove many show people, who were suffering hard times, from the business forever.

In 1940, the showman and holiday camp pioneer Billy Butlin was summoned to Downing Street and asked to get fairs open again, to boost the Nations morale. Local authorities then encouraged fairs to open once more. The older generation may recall that this was the start of the "Holiday At Home Fairs" and, with severe lighting restriction they were often called 'blackout' fairs. Showmen eligible to fight were called up, like everyone else, so manpower was drained from fairgrounds, yet the fairs were under pressure to stay open. Although those too old or too young to fight kept everything going, fairs were running at only one-fifth of the pre-war period.

This book tells of a forgotten but fascinating aspect of the war: how showmen's food, fuel and prizes were rationed, how shooting galleries overcame ammunition shortages and why police searched fairground living-wagons to confiscate radios. It recalls the enemy air attacks on fairs, dropping incendiaries and bombs killing or injure show families and destroy rides and living-wagons. Many rides and showmens' steam traction engines were sacrificed for munitions. Killjoys, who believed all forms of public entertainment should be stopped, also attacked fairgrounds with verbal and printed propaganda, trying to finish the business for good!

STILL THEY KEPT GOING!

In 1940, The Showmen's Guild, from monies donated by its members, presented the nation with a Spitfire aircraft for the war effort. It was named 'Fun of The Fair' and her story is recorded here. Showmen took part in the D-Day landings, and the final chapter includes stories from those veterans of their experiences. This book also covers what was happening to German showmen who were living in their own country under Nazi rule. Here is just a flavour of the fascinating stories featured in "Fairgrounds At War" which is the only book of its kind ever written on this subject. With 272 pages, it includes information from the era which has never previously been published. Illustrated with many photos and drawings.

£19.99, available by ordering at Waterstones bookshops, or send a cheque, (p&p free) to Kay Townsend, 9 Putton Lane, Charlestown, Weymouth, DT3 4AE.

Quickly selling out after it was published in 2006 and since re-printed by demand, only 800 copies are now available. This story tells how one West Country family became showmen and of their triumphs and tribulations travelling with steam engines through two World Wars and the Great Depression. Illustrated with photos. Hardback. £15.

Kay58@fsmail.net

07784733398